D1795116

the Knotting Tree

Elena Stowell, author & illustrator

Robert Prado da Fonseca, co-creator

The Knotting Tree
Copyright © 2025 Elena Stowell, story and illustrations
All Rights Reserved

This book is licensed for the purchaser's own personal enjoyment. Unauthorized reprinting of this book is prohibited and doing so constitutes U.S. copyright infringement. This book may not be reproduced in whole or in part without written permission from the copyright holder or publisher. Thank you for respecting this author's work.

First edition 2024
Published in Canton, GA, USA by thewordverve (www.thewordverve.com)

Hardback ISBN: 978-1-956856-73-6
Library of Congress Control Number: 2025900134

The Knotting Tree
A Book with Verve by *thewordverve*

Co-Creator: *Robert Prado da Fronseca*

Interior and Cover Layout by Robin Krauss
www.bookformatters.com

Our father says he'll never cut his tree down.

The bird calls are calming,

The shade is soothing,

The tree is for tying.

It's his knotting tree.

"Why do you love this tree?" Mari asks. She is the big sister to Maikon and always asking questions.

"Come here, children. I will tell you a story from our family," their *pai* (father) says.

"A tree, like this tree, grew near the home of my *avó*, your *bisavó*, great-grandmother. When she was about your age and finished her chores, she would run across the field to the tree to rest. Many times, she fell asleep.

"Animals of the sky and earth, of the jungle and water, each special in its own way, visited her dreams. She would wake up with her head filled with messages from the animals."

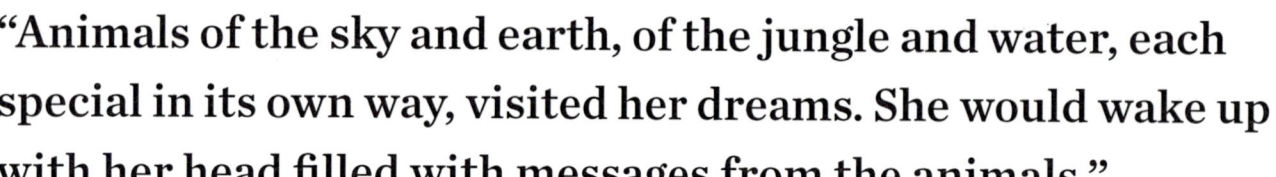

3

4

Pai's eyes sparkles as he continues, "But that's not all! *Bisavó* said the ground would be covered with animal tracks of every kind, going every which way, . . . but she never saw a single creature."

"You don't sleep under your tree," Mari points out.

"No, but the animals visit me in other ways."

Mari and Maikon are fifth-generation *sulistas*, southerners of Brazil. Their *pai* is a macrame artist.

"I didn't have much when I was a child," Pai says. "I swam in the rivers. Fished with my brothers. Chased doves from the trees."

He pauses and looks at his children. "Sometimes to *not* have is a gift."

7

Pai went on, "We played *esconde-esconde*, hide-and-seek, until our shadows disappeared and our hungry bellies led us home.

"I had freedom to explore and be myself! *Bisavó* taught me about nature's gifts. Gifts you can **hear** and **feel** and **see**."

Pai calls out to them, "Mari, Maikon . . . come! *Vem ca!*"
Brother and sister hurry to his side.

"Close your eyes and face the sun," he says. "**Hear, feel, see.**"

"I **hear** *papagaios* squawking, like too many people talking all at once," Maikon exclaims.

Mari lifts her chin and smiles. "I **feel** the sun covering me like my blanket. I am warm and safe."

"How do we see when our eyes are closed?" Maikon asks.

"You **see** nature's gifts with your heart, *querido*, (dear one)," Pai says.

Pai takes their hands. His fingers are calloused from coaxing animals from his strings. They walk back to the knotting tree.

"Did you learn to make macrame here under the tree?" Mari asks.

"First, I learned to draw by watching my brother, your uncle, tio Roger," Pai says. "Like Owl, I was observant and patient."

"I practiced, connecting lines to lines to lines.

Over time, I could see lines everywhere in nature.

Lines of minerals striping stones,

Crosshatched lines in a nest of twigs,

Curvy, circle lines made when fish kiss the water.

And the sun . . . it sends hundreds of lines connecting me to the earth."

"And you turned lines into macrame?" Maikon asks.

"Not exactly. Before you were born, I worked in a store, saving money to be ready for when you came. The road home took me past the *rua dos artesanatos*, the street where artists come together. An indigenous, *Índia*, woman there reminded me of my *avó*, grandmother. Her dreamcatchers mesmerized me with colorful strings and feathers. Those dreamcatchers grabbed a sleeping dream and woke it inside my heart. Lizard guided me to live a life inspired by that dream."

Pai tells them how each
evening, he picked up bits of
string and wire the artists left on
the ground after they'd gone home.

He added vines and feathers from the forest
to make his first dreamcatcher. It was basic, with
lumps and blunders, not as beautiful as the others he'd
seen.

But his second one was better, and the third, even better.

"We aren't always good at
doing things the first time," Pai says.
"Mouse reminds us that we must take things step by
step and pay attention to details."

20

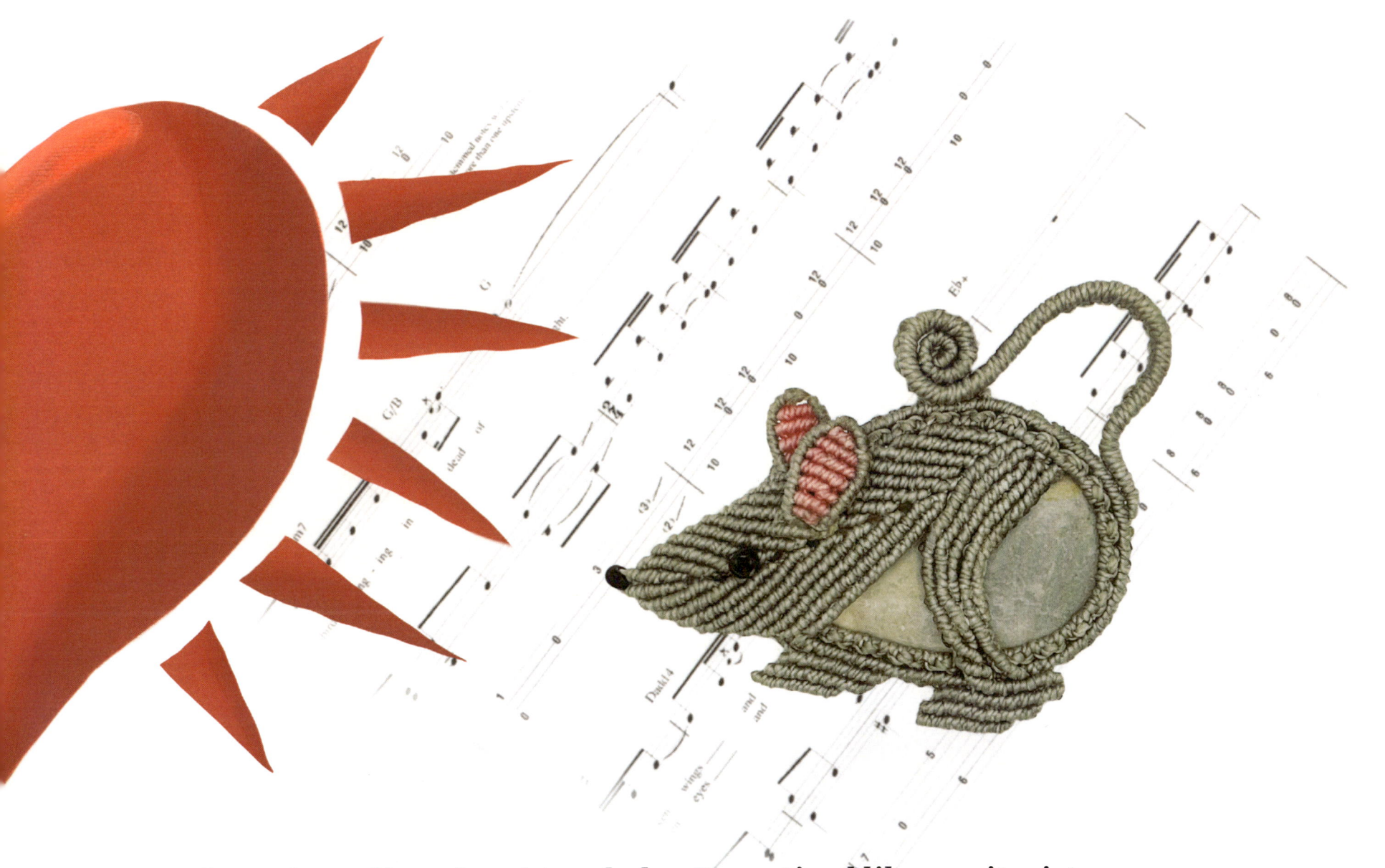

"The strings slipped and tangled as I practiced like a guitarist plucking away until a song arrived. I made simple stone pendants, *pingentes*, until, eventually, I could create from visions I had in my imagination and in my heart."

Pai explains how those visions come from Alligator wisdom, the ancient knowledge of ancestors, like Bisavó, who came before. Just as the night sky knows how to tie the stars together, this knowing without knowing, like breathing, tells his hands what to do. He draws a picture, chooses a stone, and begins to tie.

"I became like Cheetah, eager and focused to create something that didn't yet exist."

"Weren't you afraid of making mistakes?" Mari asks.

"Look up, *filha*." Pai says to his daughter. "Was the knotting tree afraid to grow this way?"

The branches go under and over, between and around, like the strings in their *pai's* macrame.

25

"Making my animals is a challenge, but a challenge is a new idea to be explored. Coatimundi teaches us to be creative problem-solvers when facing fear," their pai says.

"And if I make a mistake—" he shrugs his shoulders "—I'm still happy! Happiness chases mistakes away. My first dreamcatcher wasn't pretty, but it still caught dreams."

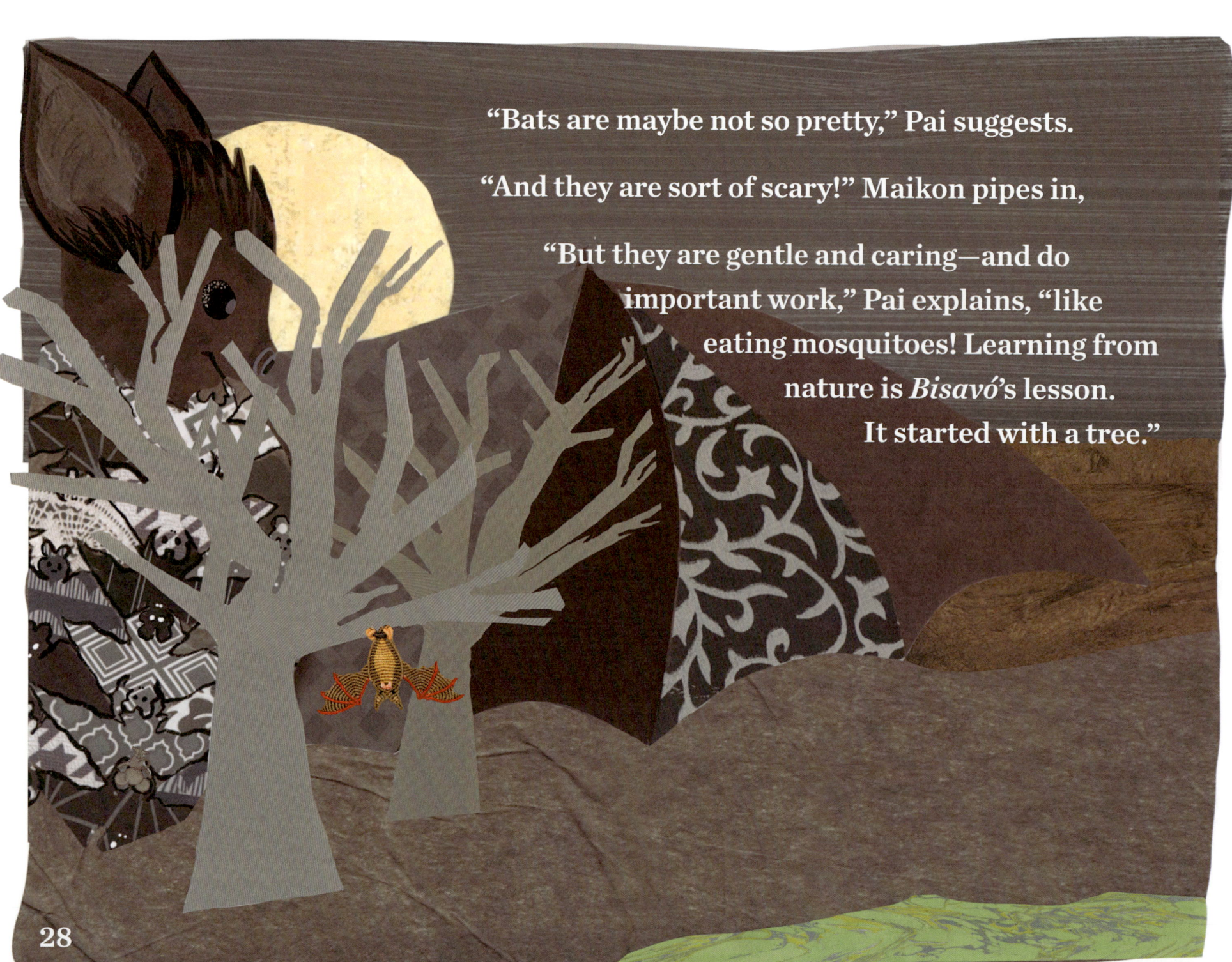

"Bats are maybe not so pretty," Pai suggests.

"And they are sort of scary!" Maikon pipes in,

"But they are gentle and caring—and do
important work," Pai explains, "like
eating mosquitoes! Learning from
nature is *Bisavó*'s lesson.
It started with a tree."

Mari thinks about her ancestors. Her *bisavó* passed these lessons on to her *avó*, and her *avó* gave them to her *pai*.

"Are you going to pass the lessons on to us?" Mari asks.

His arms wrap around Mari and Maikon. "I believe I already have. What I feel is real. My macrame brings happiness and freedom. The guidance of the animals, and you, my most precious art pieces . . . you are all real."

The children agree to be like Whale. Working together as a team to connect nature's gifts . . .

From line to line to line,

Ancestors to families,

Animals to people,

Hearts to hands.

We'll never cut Pai's tree down, Mari thinks to herself. *It's not only his knotting tree—it ties us together, too.*

About Co-Creator Robert Prado da Fonseca

Robert Prado da Fonseca, a macrame artist from a small town in Rio Grande do Sul, Brazil, grew up surrounded by the natural beauty of trees, rivers, and animals. This environment instilled in him a deep appreciation for the simplicity and interconnectedness of life, teaching him respect for all living beings.

His connection to nature is central to his work, as each knot in his macrame creations is a tribute to the animals and landscapes that inspire him. For Robert, nature is not only a home but a wise teacher whose lessons he strives to share through his art.

Robert's journey with macrame began during a period of personal crisis, when he sought a way to express his emotions and find inner peace. The act of intertwining ropes and threads became a therapeutic practice, helping him heal and transform his pain into beauty. His creations, which often incorporate elements of his gaucho culture and semi-precious stones with personal meaning, soon captured the attention of his local community. Robert believes that macrame has the power to transform lives and give purpose, and he shares this belief by teaching others the art form that helped him overcome his own struggles.

A resilient and passionate artist, Robert celebrates life, the lessons from his *avó* (grandmother), and his connection to the land and animals in every piece of macrame he creates. For him, art is a way to inspire others to respect and protect the planet, while also offering healing and self-expression.

About the Author

Elena Stowell is an award-winning author, former science teacher, and passionate Brazilian jiu-jitsu practitioner. When she isn't crafting stories, she is designing mixed-media illustrations. In her workspace, she is surrounded by paper scraps, dried paint, glue sticks, and the occasional broken toothpick, all part of her creative process. "Working in collage puts me in my happy place," she says, "even if it's a little messy."

Elena is the author of *Flowing with the Go: A Jiu-Jitsu Journey of the Soul* and the children's book *Frango & Chicken*, both stories about overcoming obstacles and finding hope despite adversity. Her latest children's book, *The Knotting Tree*, celebrates a Brazilian family's creative tradition. As co-founder of the Carly Stowell Foundation and director of the JamminBJJ Give the Gift of a Gi program, she works tirelessly to make sports and music accessible to people of all ages around the world. Through her volunteer efforts, Elena helps break down barriers, ensuring that children and adults alike have the opportunity to engage in meaningful activities.

You can learn more about Elena and follow her work at **www.elenastowell.com**

www.ingramcontent.com/pod-product-compliance
Ingram Content Group UK Ltd.
Pitfield, Milton Keynes, MK11 3LW, UK
UKRC030635020225
454448UK00001B/2